ISBN 978-0-243-08352-7
PIBN 10786008

1 MONTH OF FREE READING

at
www.ForgottenBooks.com

By purchasing this book you are eligible for one month membership to ForgottenBooks.com, giving you unlimited access to our entire collection of over 700,000 titles via our web site and mobile apps.

To claim your free month visit:
www.forgottenbooks.com/free786008

The Christian Sun.

In Essentials—Unity, In Non-Essentials—Liberty, in All Things—Charity.

ESTABLISHED 1844. GREENSBORO N. C., WEDNESDAY, OCTOBER 5, 1910. VOLUME LXII. NUMBER 40.

EDITORIAL COMMENT.

The Year 5670.—Our esteemed contemporary, The Jewish Outlook, which comes to our table every Monday and is read with more or less curious interest, celebrates in its last issue the closing of the year 5670 and the beginning of the new year 5671. It sounds strange to read editorially from a paper this time of year "We extend a very happy New Year to all our readers and trust they will grow to enjoy the Jewish Outlook more and more." etc.

There then follows a summary of events and happenings in Jewry, among Jews every where, durng the year 5670 just closing, following with this line: "We may say that on the whole the situation (for Jewry) is not bad, while it might be better. But we have hope, and we believe that the year 5671 will see greater realization of our expectations."

But then the Jewish Outlook is compelled to recognize modern—and Christian—dates for at the head and on the date line there stands, September 30, 1910.

Reverting to the year 5670. Think of a people living here amongst us for whom the Christians era has no meaning; a people in a Christian land who think back over five thousand years and have no Christ in their thinking or reckoning. How bare and bleak and desolate indeed would the years seem without the Christ, to one who is accustomed to think of those with the Christ in them. The Jews have held out long and persistently, even to their own ruin and undoing as a nation and a people; butdespite their obstinacy and resistance, the spirit of the meek and lowly One is yet to win them, for to Him every knee shall bow and every tongue confess.

A Moral Issue.—The tides of morality do not flow backwards. People may lose faith in the means of bettering moral conditions; they do not lose faith in better moral conditions themselves. If prohibition is abolished it will be solely because it does not prohibit, not because it is not a good thing. The people are determined to grapple with this liquor demon until they have mastered it and brought it into subjection. Liquor is a curse. It is a foe to the human family because so continuously and so persistently and so universally abused. If prohibition does not tame the monster then something else will be tried. The people are too enlightened and determined to go backward. In moral issues men move upwards, not downwards, forwards, not backwards. Liquor traffic means soul traffic; and men who care cannot sit idly by and see ruin wrought on every hand, without doing their best to subdue and conquer. I have not found a stronger, nor a truer word, about the saloon business than this from the Christan World:

"Just here is to be found the essence of the strongest argument against the saloon business: it is inevitably a soul traffic, more truly than was that of the old Arab slavers. It goes up in the scale of prosperity only as souls go down in the scale of humanity. It thrives on ruin. It no more surely requires chrushed apples to make cider than it requires crushed lives to make saloon profits. It treats men as things to be exploited, as jumping jacks to perform their fantastic antics to gratify others' whims. It ignores completely the higher brotherly relation, and crushes all of the humanity out of men for the sake of cash."

Leaving The Ministry.—The dispatches announce that at one of the Annual Conferences of the M. E. Church the other day fifty-two preachers asked to be released in order to engage in secular pursuits. The dispatch goes on to say that low salaries were the cause of the defection, and that the retiring ministers were efficient, well equiped, and were meeting the demands of their constituency. What is occurring in the Conference named is taking place, to greater or less degree, in other conferences and connections.

This may seem a sad state of affairs, and is, but to our thinking the ministry is better off without these men and their kind. We are not upholding the custom of low salaries paid to preachers—lower than to any other class of laborers with the same amount of preparation and equipment. Despite this fact, the preacher who is in earnest about it, who feels duty bound to preach, who feels that he must preach, that God has called him to preach will not quit and go into secular pursuits, purely for the money. There are other and higher considerations for the minister o fthe right type, and he will not quit. He has made the start. He has put his hands to the plow. There is no turning back with him. He is enamored of his calling. He knows that the ministry is the highest and holiest calling a man ever was honored with. He knows there are greater possibilities for good and for usefulness for him in the ministry than there are anywhere else on earth. And he wll not quit. He does not ask to be "released." He only asks opportunity for further service. And such a minister knows well enough that the public whom he serves will learn and will know of his work. The world, as well as the church, knows that the laborer is worthy of his hire.

There are not riches for the minister, neither indeed should there be. A rich minister is not worth hearing in the pulpit. But there ever has been, there ever will be, a living, a decent and honorable living, support, and comfortable support for the right sort of minister. And the minister needs no other than the called and the chosen according to His purpose.

LIFE OF JAMES O'KELLY.

Dear Dr. Atkinson:—I have just finished reading with pleasure and profit the Life of James O'Kelly by McClenny. The book is well written and handsomely bound. One is impressed as he reads, that McClenny searched long and carefully for facts. This book deals with facts, and those who read these facts will be impressed that they are studying the history of a man who lived far in advance of his fellows in Christian liberty and church polity. All honor to McClenny for this book. My love has been made stronger for the Christian Church. H. W. Elder.

Richland, Ga.

—Thirty seven persons were killed and twenty injured in a collision between two street cars near Staunton, Ill. Oct. 4. The failure to obey orders is assigned as the sole cause of the awful tragedy.

FROM THE FIELD.

Winchester Letter.

It was my pleasure last week to be with Bro. C. E. Newman at Liberty church, Vance County, N. C. I taught school there one year and it was quite a pleasure to meet so many old friends and acquaintances. Uncle Wellons was there and rendered valuable service. Dr. Herudon was also present and assisted in several services. Bro. Newman is held in high esteem by the church and community.

The Lord graciously blessed us in the services and many were converted and reclaimed and set their faces Zionward.

The Ladies' Aid Society at Winchester has purchased a handsome new organ for use in our services. The brick are being delivered for the veneer on our new building.

The following contributions have been received:

Previously reported	$2024.62
Miss Lydia Creswell	10.00
A. B. Richards	10.00
Dr. J. L. Whitlock	5.00
E. P .Louderback	5.00
Cash Collection (Winchester)	2.78
J. E. Watkins	8.00
J. A. Kagey	2.00
Rent	4.00
J. H. Himler	1.67
Mrs. A. H. Liskey	3.00
Zebedee Marshall	5.00
L. C. Morris	1.00
L. S. Johnson	20.00
Wm. Eaton	1.00
A. D. Larrick	5.00
Mrs. Virginia Morris	1.00
H. P. Hook	10.00
C. E. Society (Timber Ridge)	13.82
Thos. L. Larick	5.00
T. L. Deavers	3.33
Mrs. Fannie Zirele	1.00
Rev. A. W .Andes	1.67
Jerry Thorpe	2.00
Mrs. J. W. Tate	3.00
Miss Emma Fulk	2.00
Mrs. W. M. Serickler	10.00
W. J. Estep	5.00
Mrs. E. L. Moffitt	2.00
Bernarda Shifflett	1.67
B. L. Nichols	1.00
C. W. Houck	5.00
Total	$2175.56

We are thankful for all these contributions. We are still needing funds for carrying on the work. May we count on you to send your contribution now?

W. T. Walters.

Chipley, Ga., Letter.

I have only one more visit to my churches before Conference and, with the arrangements already made. I feel sure I shall find them ready.

Ready! I did not think of that until it was written. That is a serious thought; ready. My idea was that my churches would have all the Conference apportonment for missions, ministerial education, etc. Well, that is all right. The work of the conference would not succeed without it. But to be "ready" in time for the "Conference" will require special efforts. After all, that is the only successful kind of life—being ready.

My work for this year has been of peculiar interest to me. Mt. Zion, where I am closing my third year as pastor, has succeeded, I think real well. Every thing has gone along smoothly and, as results of our efforts we have received fourteen members into the church this year. There is a very bright prospect for the church and community.

This is my first year with the people at Lanett, but considering circumstances to begin with we have had a very pleasant year. Both the Sunday school and congregations at preaching services have increased threefold; and I have received nineteen members into the church.

I am closing my second year with the Langdale church. We have good congregations and I feel that we have advanced spiritually and in membership. We have received nineteen members here also.

If I had told you how I had received my members you would have agreed with me in my first statement. Out of the fifty-two members received there have been only twenty-one applicants for baptism. But I rejoice that so many have been reclaimed and others have brought their letters from their accustomed place—the trunk.

Let's pray for another good session of Conference this year.

E. M. Carter.

Burlington.

We have just closed an interesting protracted meeting with the Burlington Christian Church. It lasted fifteen days, beginning on the 11the of Sept. and closing on the 25th. Rev. H. W. Elder of Richland, Ga., reached us on the 13th and remained till the morning of the 23rd.

He did all the preaching during his stay. Bro. Elder is a good revivalist. His sermons are interesting and instructive. His personal fund of illustrations is abundant, and when told in his own touching way, tug mightily at the heart and touch the deep issues of life.

Bro. Leon Smith, the popular pastor of the Graham Christian Church was with us three nights, and preached twice—on the thirl and 25th. His sermons were good and well received.

There were thirty-five or forty professions during the meeting, and on last Sunday, the 25th, received seventeen into the church fellowship. I have the names of others who contemplate joining.

Prior to the meeting I sent out nearly three hundred pastoral letters, in which I urged united and persistent prayer. The letters received from nonresident members bore many kind words, and they all breathed an earnest prayer for God's blessings to rest upon the services.

The communion services at the beginning of the meeting was largely attended. I think it was the largest communion service that I have witnessed with the church, during my pastorate. On Sunday morning, the 18th, we had roll call, and some who could not be present, sent letters and other verses of Scripture to be read when their nam s were called. We had a good meeting, and our hearts go out to God in profound thanks.

P. H. Fleming, Pastor.

Holland, Va.

Th annual protracted meeting was held the week following the 3rd Sunday in Sept. Dr. W. W. Staley did the preaching in his own peculiar style—practical, clear and forceful—and it was much enjoyed by the large congregations. Ther were eleven professions, ten joined the church, and nine were baptized.

N. G. Newman.

APPOINTMENTS IN ALABAMA CONFERENCE.

Rev. Leon E. Smith, who goes to Alabama and Georgia to represent The Christian Sun and our Book Depository will preach at the following places and times:

Beulah, Thursday night, Oct. 20th.
Mt. Zion, Friday night, Oct. 21st.
New Hope, Sat, & Sun., 22nd &23rd.

Appointments arranged by,

Rev. G. D. Hunt.

Will those interested kindly make these appointments known? And will Sun subscribers, and friends of their church paper, please see Bro. Smith at one or the other of these appointments?

J. O. A.

—China has presented to the United States an encyclopedia of 5,000 volumes published in 1736. It takes 600 cases of the Congressional Library to hold it.

McCLENNY'S LIFE OF REV. JAMES O'KELLY.

What Some Who Have Read It are Saying about It.

The greatest book ever published by the Christian Church is McClenny's Life of Rev. James O'Kelly and the Early History of the Christian Church in the South. No member of the Christian Church in America or Canada should fail to have this book at once. —Hon. J. E. West, Member of the General Assembly, Suffolk, Va.

I read the "Life of Rev. James O'Kelly" is less than 24 hours after receiving it. To me it read like a romance, not only because he is very likely one of my ancestors, but because of the facts connected with the struggle he made for religious freedom in church government etc. You have done your own denomination, The Christian Church, a service, and in so doing you have served the lovers of religious freedom.—Rev. N. B. O'Kelly, Baptist minister of Dawson, Ga.

Immediately on seeing that your book was ready for delivery I ordered it from the Christian Sun. It came yesterday morning and I have been devouring it. You have indeed done a great work for the Christian denomination in the cause of truth. I have not read quite a hundred pages yet, but can scarcely lay the book aside.—Rev. J. F. Burnett, Sect. of A. C. C., Dayton, O.

I have recently read with much pleasure and profit the valuable work of our townsman, Mr. W. E. McClenny, entitled "The Life of Rev. James O'Kelly." I found the work full of interesting and instructive matter. It deserves a place in every well appointed library, and should certainly be in the hands of every member of the Christian Church, who desires to know something of the early struggle and history of his denomination.—Ex-Judge R. H. Rawls, attorney-at-law and Notary-Public, Suffolk, Va.

I purchased McClenny's "Life of Rev. James O'Kelly" recently and have already read a part of it with intense interest.—Rev. H. E. Rountree, Waverly, Va.

On every hand our people are talking and reading about McClenny's "Life of Rev. James O'Kelly." No wonder. It contains more facts about why and how the Christian Church began in the South than were ever collected in any one book before. It is full of historical information of the most vital sort.—Windsor, Va., Correspondence of Suffolk Herald.

I have just recently been able to read McClenny's new book, "The Life of Rev. James O'Kelly," and I am delighted with it. It is well written, reads as though the author might have had several other books to his credit. There's not a dull page in it, for it is full of interesting facts and conditions from start to finish.

I regard the book as one of the best biographies I have read in a long time. Considering the obstacles he must have met with in gathering his material, on account of the long years that have elapsed since Mr. O'Kelly's death, and the fact that so little has been written about him, I think Mr. McClenny has really given us a remarkable book, and it is not simply a biography of James O'Kelly—it is a splendid history of the origin and early years of the Christian Church. The book ought to be read by every member of the Christian Church. Our people owe McClenny a debt of gratitude for his tireless efforts in preparing this most valuable addition to our church literature.—Pres. E. L. Moffitt, Elon College, N. C.

The Life of Rev. James O'Kelly, the leader and pioneer in the organization of the Christian Church, by Mr. W. E. McClenny shows a great deal of original research, a careful collecting of historical facts, the organization of these facts about the life of the leading character and the production of a history that will be of permanent value to the church. It is well worthy of a place in the thought and library of every minister and member of the denomination; because it reveals the cause, struggles, persecutions, and conditions that gave being to a church without human dogma, untrameled in conscientious convictions and free from the galling yoke of ecclesiastical oppression.—Dr. W. C. Wicker, Elon College, N. C.

O'Kelly's Life by McClenny, if written seventy-five years ago, would have meant for us as a people to-day many times as many members as we now have. For in the compass of his two hundred and fifty pages he has very satisfactorily answered all of the charges of heresy brought by the enemies of religious liberty against our infant brotherhood, and he has done this in the only sure way, by documentary evidence.

It is but natural in a pioneer work of this kind that there should be some ground for difference of opinion on minor points, but is remarkable with what steadfastness of foresight the author has analyzed the mass of material at his command and done a real creative work in bringing order out of chaos, with so little ground for disagreement. It is true no doubt that James O'Kelly at first regarded the organization he headed as a Methodist body shorn of its bishop and presiding elders. But the idea grew on, him, as every forward movement for freedom, whether civil or ecclesiastical has always done, until he would not have been willng to go back into the Methodist Church, even though bereft of its episcopacy and supplied with a republican form of government. Be that as it may, the Christian Church today is far more than the Methodist Church, with a republican or congregational form of government.

The second edition of this excellent work, a work of permanent value and real and vital contribution not only to our own church history, but to general church history as well, will certainly contain an index. It will also be greatly helped by the addition of a chapter setting forth more completely the principles of our Church as held by us today. MacClenny has done a noble work for his brethren, and they will record their approval and appreciation by speedily exhausting the first edition. I commend the book most earnestly to all lovers of truth and fairness, whether of the Christian persuasion or not.

. W. A. Harper.

Elon College. N. C., 9-28-1901. .

—The postal receipts for Aug. at Chicago, $1,666,484, led all American cities, New York being $56,000 behind. Chicago's increase over the corresponding month of last year was 19 percent, while New York gained on 11.6 per cent.—Ex.

—In Russia the year's tale of deaths is 88,714 out of 191,076 cases. The zone of infection now includes remote sections of Siberia. The number of new cases now averages 4,000 a week. Barely half yet admit the presence of the disease, the patients recover. Naples will not but on September 23 the cable reported fifty cases there and thirty deaths.—Ex.

—In the brief and crowded annals of aviation there has been no such feat of daring as that of George Chavez—native of France and resident of Peru— who on Friday, September 23, rose from Brieg in Switzerland on a monoplane to a height of a mile and a half and then flew unerringly over the rugged Simplon Alps, where descent would have been death and came down at Domo d'Ossola in Italy. The distressing, and perhaps fatal mishap which ended his alighting must not be allowed to dim the glory of that first transalpine flight.—Ex.

NOTES AND PERSONALS.

—The foot-ball season opened Saturday and there were many games. Here is hoping that the boys who opened the season will scape with their necks to see it close; but the awful tragedies of the last season make us fear and dread for them.

—It is said that Rev. Chas. M. Sheldon, author of "In His Steps, or, What Would Jesus Do?" is dramatizing that book and is to put it on the stage. We sincerely hope that the report is untrue, as such a performance would be sheer sacrilege.

—Rev. W. S. Long, D. D., one of the strong preachers of the South, is open to an engagement, as pastor. He has had a long experience in the pastorate, and we commend to our people in want of a pastor the consideration of this opportunity for securing a strong man. Address Rev. W. S. Long, Graham, N. C. —Herald of Gospel Liberty.

—We are sincerely trusting that the political corruption of the 2nd Virginia district will not infect its fine oysters—the very finest and best on earth. For these savory bivalves to become infected, as the politics of the district have, would be a national calamity. Will the esteemed Norfolk Landmark graciously see to it that its oysters at least are kept pure. At present all else thereabouts seems hopeless.

—Do not think that because your own Sunday school lags and lingers and does not grow that the Sunday school as such is passing out. Not by any manner of means. Mr. Marion Lawrence, General Secretary of the International Sunday School Association, in his annual report says that Sunday schools are now growing at the rate of two hundred schools with 20,000 new members, every Sunday.

—We were just going to say that if Dr. Staley did not come along with Suffolk letter we never would let him go fishing with us again in Bro. Beale Johnson's mill-pond; but the Doctor comes in this week and his Suffolk letter looks so good, and reads so good, and closes so nicely, that we withdraw the threat and keep open the invitation as long as he keeps up the letters. Now if that will not fetch him nothing will.

—Mr. and Mrs. R. H. Elliott, formerly of Norfolk, now of Ocean View ,Va have issued invitations to the marriage of their daughter, Miss Alma, to Dr. Rowland Daniel Wolfe Wednesday, Oct. 12, 1910. The newly married pair will reside at Council Grove, Kansas, being at home there after Nov. 15. Miss Alma was a student at Elon and has many

friends here. She has our best wishes and Dr. Wolfe our heartiest congratulations.

—We trust that Bro. Howsare, pastor of Memorial Temple, Norfolk, will enjoy a gracious revival. He has been laboring with great efficiency and faithfulness in the Norfolk work the past year and we trust he is to see now some of the fruits of the year's toil. We once heard Dr. Staley say that he believed the conversion of souls in a congregation was the Lord's seal of approval of the minister's service. Bro. Howsare's meeting is to continue from Oct. 2 to 16, and he is being assisted by Rev. M. J. Swearingen of Delaware, Ohio.

—We are printing elsewhere just a few of the many words of praise and commendation MacClenny's life of Rev. James O'Kelly is receiving. Sun reader, you can not afford not to secure and read this book. It contains more history of the Christian Church, and more historical facts about O'Kelly than were ever gathered in one volume before. People who read the book are surprised and delighted. The candid conviction of those who read the book is that it will do them more good than any book ever published so far to set before the world in its proper light the Christian Church in the South. The book sells for $1.50 postpaid and may be ordered either of the author at Suffolk, Va., or The Christian Sun, Elon College, N. C.

—Plesant Grove Church, Halifax Co., Va., is one of the few country churches we know which has a baptismal pool under its roof. Draw a curtain and throw back the large folding doors in rear of the pulpit and the congregation may witness from their seats the beautiful solemn service of baptism by immersion. The water is supplied the pool through gutters that drain the roof when there is rain. The arrangement is simple and comparatively inexpensive, and the service is beautiful, solemn, impressive. The wonder is that so many of our country congregations will put themselves to so much inconvenience and then frequently have to baptize in a stream or hole that is muddy or unclean, when to make a convenient and wholesome arrangement would cost so little.

—The Muncie Christian Church, if we mistake not, has ninety per cent of its members giving according to the Scriptural method—tithing, and Bro. Stockley declares that under that system the finances of the church are flourishing—that all bills are paid and money is in the treasury for any unexpected need. Notwithstanding all this the members of the Muncie church are living and as comfortable, no doubt, as they were before

tithing, and yet they are giving much more to the cause of Christ. This act of obedience is most important. We wish all of our churches would adopt the tithing plan, for no doubt it is not only the best way to finance the church, but even more than this, it is God's way of doing it.—Editor J. P. Barett in Herald of Gospel Liberty.—Amen and amen.

—The editor had the happy privilege of laboring four days of last week—Monday to Thursday—in a series of meetings with Pastor J. W. Holt, at Union Ridge, Alamance Co., N. C. The people of Union have built a magnificent house of worship, and furnished it handsomely and comfortably. They have shown their care and concern for the Lord's work in their midst by a liberal outlay of their substance and the Lord is blessing their liberality. The people are justly proud of their beautiful concrete house with its solid, circular oak pews and its windows of cathedral glass, and they love their church and its service. They were ready for the meeting and entered into its spirit with zeal. There must have been thirty or more conversions, fourteen joining the church on Wednesday p. m., and eight Thursday. Bro. Holt is much beloved by his people and he is enjoying the good work there. There are signs of church loyalty, growth and development on every hand. Congregations are good, growing and attentive. It was a pleasure indeed to be with them in their good and glorious revival.

APPOINTMENTS IN ALABAMA CONFERENCE.

Rev. L. E. Smith, will preach at the following points on dates named, and will also represent the Christian Sun:

Beulah, Thursday night, Oct. 20.

Mt Zion, Friday night, Oct. 21.

New Hope, Saturday and Sunday, Oct. 22 and 23.

Antioch, Sunday night, Oct. 23.

Appointments made by Rev. G. D. Hunt.

Will members of these churches who may see this notice, make the appointments known and oblige?   J. O.A.

APPOINTMENTS IN GA. & ALA. CONFERENCE.

Rev. Leon E. Smith will preach at the following places, and represent the Sun:

Beulah, Wednesday night, Oct. 26.

Rose Hill (Columbus) Thurs. night, Oct. 27.

Brown Springs, Friday night, Oct. 28.

Red Hill, Saturday night Oct. 29.

Richland, Sunday, 11 a. m.& 7:30 p.m.

Langdale, Monday night, Oct. 31.

La Nett, Tuesday night, Nov. 1.

Oak Grove, Wernesday, 11 a. m., Nov. 2.

LaGrange. Wednesday night, Nov. 2.

Appointments made by Rev. H. W. Elder.

NORFOLK LETTER.

, Prospects are bright for a good meeting at the Memorial Temple.

Rev. M. J. Swearingen of Delaware, Ohio, arrived in the. city Saturday. He is a preacher of rare ability and a good singer and knows how to get others to sing. The beginning was encouraging yesterday. Congregations were good and especially at night when they had the house nearly filled. After a stirring service there were two conversions.

This is a critical time in the life of the Memorial Temple. Let the brotherhood at large unite in their prayers with those of the brethren laboring here that this shall be a great meeting, for such a meeting would mean much to the work at this point for the future. Bro. Swearingen also preached at Rosemont in the afternoon. Bro. Howsare assisted Dr. Booker, of Epworth Church, in the funeral of Robt. K. Haynes. The deceased was a brother of the late John C. Haynes and of Mrs. E. J. Brickhouse.

He died very suddenly. He leaves a wife besides a large numbr of relatives. They have the sympathy of a large circle of friends.

The meetings in progress at Lamberts Point are reported as being very good with some conversions, but I have not learned how many up to this time.

The bi-monthly meeting of the ministers of the E. Va. Conference meets today in the study of the pastor of Memorial Temple. They are to study the "Life of Paul."

A large attendance is expected.

J. W. Manning.

GYMNASIUM AT ELON COLLEGE.

Friends, students and villagers have done well. The Gymnasium fund now amounts to more than $300.00. This is a splendid beginning, but we still need your support, and your enthusiasm.

Now let every one who has a care for the well being at Elon College, put a shoulder to the wheel, and give to our school, the greatest asset of the Christian Church, our money and our encouragment.

If you can send a letter of advise and encouragement—and best of all a donation—let it come along. Make yourselves happy, and us glad.

E. T. Hines,
Chman. of Committee.

CONFERENCE NOTICES.
Notice.

All ministers, delegates and visitors who expecte to attend the Eastern Va. Conference which meets at Main Street Christian Church, Berkely Ward, Norfolk, Va., Nov. 1st to 4th, will please notify the pastor, Rev. M. L. Bryant,
33 Poplar Ave.,
Berkley, Va.

A GOOD FINANCIAL BACKING.

"Be you the women that's. tryin' to help folks?"

There was a smudge or two on the face of the inquirer, a newsboy of ten or eleven, who with a bundle of papers still under his arm, had found his way into our office. But the smudges had no chance at all against the genuine benignity that beamed from every lineament.

"Why, yes, we try to help people."

There was a grunt of satisfaction and a tug at a bulging pocket, from which was extracted, with some little trouble, a stout paper bag, tightly fastened at the end. Tim undid the bag and with an inimitable flourish of prodigality flung a whole dollar in pennies upon the table.

"There!" he breathed. "We guys thought we'd like to help you, so we chipped in. And if you want any more, just call on us."—Deaconess Advocate.

MATTING INDUSTRY IN CHINA.

The experiments which are now being carried on with a view to establishing the reed-growing industry in the United States for the making of matting lends interest to facts regarding the matting industry in China presented by United States Vice-Consul-General Myers ,of Canton. This country receives annually from China about 50,000,000 square yards of matting, an importation which may in time be considerably curtailed—if the aforementioned experiments are successful—to the injury of large numbers of people in Southern China, who now find in the manufacture of matting their chief means of livelihood. The straw seed is planted in sheltered spots, and a few months later transplanted into fields previously covered with water. Women and children generally perform the work of splitting the harvested reeds and laying them out in the sun to dry. The straw for matting is carefully assorted for quality and size, the cheaper grades being used in dyeing. Men do all the work at the looms in the making of the better styles of matting, which come from the Lintan district, about two hundred miles to the west of Canton. Most of the matting used in the United States comes from the Tung Kun district, whence it is sent to Canton for inspection by the foreign exporter before shipment.—Selected.

AGITATION FOR CHRISTIAN UNION.

The Dnyamodaya makes suggestion toward interdenominational approachment, seconding one made by the Bombay Guardian. Our contemporary says, "Surely every mission at its regular and also at its occasional special gatherings could with great profit invite representatives from other missions to give the best inspiration of their beliefs and the best counsel of their experiences on various problems of thought and administration. Every mission's successful attempt and the failures, too, can furnish helpful suggestions to other workers in the same field, or can evoke helpful suggestions from those who have been more successful." We fully agree with our contemporary in saying that "personal intercourse can do more than can published ideas and reports, criticisms and approbations, toward that mutual understanding, mutual appreciation, mutual suffering, mutual inspiration and an effective cooperation which are needed for the joyful and successful prosecution of Christian work. Such interchange of friendly visits need not wait for the formation of any organization. Indeed, they may be the most efficacious means of consummating a formal union. At any rate, they would be not difficult and yet valuable means of Christian fellowship and Christian service." The only proviso we should ask for is that these interchanges should be recognized as thoroughly informal rather than official. The more we know of each other the better.—Indian Witness.

—The Times (newspaper) building of Los Angeles, Cal., was wrecked by an explosion Saturday a .m., last, nineteen bodies being buried under the debris. It is believed that Union printers blew up the building, they having a grudge against the proprietor who refused to employ Union labor.

—The State Fair management has established this year special contests for corn growers and cotton growers, for men and boys, offering large prizes, as much as $100.00 for the best corn grown by a. man, and $100.00 for the best corn grown by a boy under eighteen. Samples are to on exibition at the Fair during the week of October 17-22. All particulars as to these contests will promptly be furnished on application to the Secretary, Joseph E. Pogue, Raleigh, N. C.

PRACTICE.

This word, briefly defined, means frequent use, exercise, to do. The first consideration presents itself in the question, What do you practice? A daily practice is kept up by every one, and it is doing something or it is doing nothing. No one can escape the searching investigation of this truth. Whether it is admitted or not, it is practically so. Regular, earnest practice produces more proficiency in any thing by making stronger every part brought into exercise, and he who would gain the best and greatest success must practice diligently. Good practices ought to be encouraged, and refraining from bad ones is the right thing to do. What a great improvement and a wonderful development is noticed in the growth in grace as the Christian practices his profession by cultivating the fruits of the spirit. When the mind, soul, and heart are practicing under the influence of the Spirit there is a more lovely and admirable expression —a fulness and tenderness in the voice, a sweet and lovable deportment and an attractiveness which did not exist before. Go into the halls of fame and look at the silent marble lips and the beaming face of some Christian man or woman whose life was brilliant, bright and beautiful, and you still feel their silent influence as you think of their greatness and goodness. They impressed you as immortal beings still living on earth in well carved statuary, and, at the same time, living the life everlasting. Therefore living here and hereafter as monuments of right living, and of industrious practice in those things which made their lives sublime.

Some practice all the opposition they can to religious influences. Even some so-called great ones attack the Bible and its doctrine with the weakest reason that a poor weak, sinful doubter can produce. They may have a few followers of the weaker and baser kind, but their lasting influence will be felt in the Christian world as much as a fly is felt on an elephant's tusk. The cause of right, justice and truth will stand forever, but the cause of the liar and foolish will not stand the test of reason and religion.

The fruits of the Spirit are the things to cultivate and practice. Think them over—study them, look for and learn them well; practice them every day and there will soon be noticed signs of great improvement in your spiritual condition. It is not hard to do your duty, if you will practice it. These fruits of the Spirit will become

so lovable, you will really like them more all the time. The works of the flesh you have done so often, leave them and cultivate the spirit, and realize how much better you are. Begin now, practice them, and you and others too will take special notice that you have been with God. It is not strange that so many sweet, winsome, expressive and impressive faces are seen among the consecrated servants of the Lord. Their themes are lofty, their thoughts are heavenly, and their conception of His love is so wonderful. They practice communion with God, and, like Moses, they shine with the brightness of His glory. In my hearing recently a fine Christian character said to another devoted follower of Jesus, You look different from others, and your face appears to gleam with a lovely radiance and inexpressible pleasure. They went and told Jesus. You go and tell Him all about yourself and invite Him to abide with you.

In the cheerless hours of trouble when no one is nigh to comfort, He lovingly whispers, Let not your heart be troubled.   J. T. Kitchen.

OF SUCH IS THE KINGDOM OF HEAVEN.

It is no wonder that the Lord sometimes opens the character of children quickly and then takes them to Himself—no wonder, because to begin with children are more nearly ready for ripening than men and women.

One day He stood looking down into the eyes of a child, who looked up into His with perfect confidence and said: "Of such is the kingdom of heaven." How could he keep out of heaven one who was ready for it and hence what wonder that we lose our ripe children and keep to train those who, perhaps, because of loss of confidence must ripen more slowly?

It was only a few days ago that the blessed One, who stood in the streets of the Eastern village, came and looked into the eyes of a little girl in one of our own cities and said: "Of such is the kingdom of heaven," and beckoning she went back with Him, because she was all ready to go.

Ruth was a child who years ago became acquainted with the ministering Angel Pain, and this blessed messenger of God taught her so many things that other children do not know that the Jesus of Galilee had to come to a little Pennsylvania city to take her home to heaven.

The Angel Pain told Ruth one day that it would be nice to try and make her

father and mother forget that she had to wear a heavy brace. So she never referred to it herself, and was cheery and even happy when the little limb had to be painfully treated. And so Ruth and the pain Angel ripened the sweet-tasting fruit of patience, which even men and women rarely produce in perfection.

At another time the Pain Angel said: "If you want to forget your pain just think what you can do for somebody else, for Jesus' sake." So many times, with great difficulty, she found out and visited old people and "shut-ins," and didn't tell anybody about it, and even her parents didn't know until after she had gone home how many people would miss the visits of little Ruth.

One lady has written her mother: "She seemed to come to me like a bright sunbeam, adding to my life a bright spot which was all her own. It seems to me in the last few days I have recalled every incident of our acquaintance, I loved her and enjoyed her so much."

Only a week before she bade good-by to this earth she urged her mother to attend to the buying of books and toys and fruit to take to the postman's child who had just been stricken in like manner. Her father and mother went to the house on Saturday evening, and when they returned Ruth showed great interest in their visit and description of the family, and when all was told seemed entirely satisfied.

Ruth organized a branch of the Busy Bee Culb, and began at once to work for the children of the general hospital in her home city. While planning for a porch party and sale she was taken ill, and although confined to her bed most of the day, she spent her time maturing the plans. When the day came for the affair she was hardly able to be up, but was allowed to sit on the porch and to enjoy the success of the labors of her little companions, which amounted in money to $46. Two days before she passed away she told her loved ones she wanted to make up the amount to $50 by adding some money which had been promised her by the physician under a little contract which he had with her concerning some incident of her disease. The fact that she was able to claim the $5 did not seem as important to her in the matter of her recovery as was the hope that she might increase the hospital fund. When the local paper gave her more credit for the success of the sale than she thought she deserved, she burst into tears. The other girls wanted to wait until she might be able to go with them to present the money to the hospital, but she urged that they go without her ,as she had already had too much credit.

And so Ruth was ripening in unselfishness, thoughtfulness, sympahty, modesty and even in patience until Jesus came to her and said: "It is enough; come up higher," and the two went home together.—N. Y. Christian Advocate.

THE FLOODS IN JAPAN.

Ishinomaki, Japan,
Aug. 31, 1910.

Dear Sun Readers:

Many of you will have read about the great flood which visited Japan this month and will want to know the condition around our churches.

I have not heard from the most northern church, Ichinoseki, but the river there is said to be 28 feet high, and people who have second stories use them for embarking in the river by boat as the first story is flooded.

About half the city is said to be covered with water.

In Tsukidate and Wakayanagi little harm was done and the Wakayanagi pastor with his bicycle was ahead of the American, in reaching the scene of worst disaster That is Iwadeyama, where is our youngest church of twelve members.

I visited there last week. About 50 persons have died, 28 houses were totally destroyed, 51 houses half ruined and over 400 houses injured by water and sand. The houses are poorly built anyway and the most lasting injury, to those whose friends are still safe, is to the crops.

Miss Ueno told me that their rice crop is wholly ruined—not only that, but what they had on hand they had to give to keep the people from starving around them.

The brother, not yet a Christian, and knowing his crop was ruined, gave 8 koker of rice to the sufferers. (One koku is 158 quarts.)

A pretty generous gift for a man not a Christian – even under such distressing circumstances.

The Christians are themselves safe and trying to help as they can in the distress around them.

I helped as I could, and in reportng to the Ishinomaki church my visit last Sunday, they appointed a committee to raise funds to send to Iwadeyama.

Our city suffered less than any other part of Miyagi Ken.

Four fifths of the crop in Miyagi Ken is said to be ruined. Fortunately the treasurer of our church who a week ago had supposed that his rice crop was ruined finds it is not, and the rice crop

will not equal that of a good year. But the salt fields, about which I wrote in my last letter have suffered temporary disaster—which means no work during the rainy days and no regular work while the fields are being repaired.

In Wakuya, the dyke was cut to save the town, and the water turned off.

Our pastor packed his goods in boxes, stored them up in the high rafters and prepared for flight. But a different section of dyke was cut and that part of Wakuya suffered not at all. Mrs. Sakurai was sheltering two people whose house was still flooded, as I passed through last week.

Good old grandmother Ito, 85 years old, lives in one room of a long tenement house beside the dyke. She was taken for safety to a neighbor's, but the house was not flooded as was expected. We are all so grateful that she was kept safe. While visiting there with the pastor a little six-year-old appeared begging. "O Miss Tiger, where did you come from? Where have you been?" they cried. She looked anything but tiger-like, though she ate the cold dumpling and red beans they gave her with her fingers about as animals would.

On inquiry it seems that she had been abandoned by her mother some years ago and the grandmother who had sometimes been seen begging with her, disappeared during the flood.

The people with whom she had stayed the night before were glad to give her to us, saying they had no responsibility for her, so I called a kouruma and took her home. She is very quiet and obedient. When she recovers from the whooping-cough, and when the mayor has finished his search for her relatives, I suppose, since she is too far away to send to "Uncle Jim and Aunt Myrtle," at Elon College "up on the hill," that she should be sent to the Union Sendai Orphanage.

Our people promised 125 yen as our part to that orphanage, but I very much fear we've not been able to give it this year.

Can't you add in your offering for Foreign Missions something to make it possible for us to do for this little girl what we believe the Master would have us do? Probably $20 a year will support her. That allows $1.50 a month for food and $2 a year for clothes and extras.

This morning Mr. Ito, the richest man in Kanomata village, called to ask my help for two villages near his. They have both been destroyed, he says. He "commanded" 500 men from his village and they marched like an army (Mr.

Ito is a university graduate and uses English on the dykes and saved their own village so that not even the crops are injured.

But these villages around with a population of 3,000 are still being cared for by the town. A rice ball called "omu-sube," is given them for each meal. Of course it is not enough, but it keeps them from starving.

"My mother has given everything from my farm to those people. We have nothing on it now," Mr. Ito said.

I promised to visit the town offices with him next Friday, gather clothing and help as I can.

As he went away he said, "Every night we hear the children across the river crying for food.

The south suffered also and Mrs. Watanabe (whose family some churches in Va. supported for a time) swam out of the five feet of water which flooded her home and so saved her life.

But others will write of that. There are still broken tracks here and there so that mail and other traffic is still but it is improving all the time.

Here is a large opportunity for us to exercise Christian charity indeed to lead the charitable forces.

These people were becoming proud of their victory with Russia and influence in Corea and saying that the spirit of bushido (chivalry) was better than Christianity.

The flood will not be wholly an evil if it softens hearts and brings many to seek the unchanging God of Mercy and Justice.

Pray and work for us that we may use this special opportunity to its utmost for Him.

Alice M. True.

NOTICE.

To the members of the Western N. C. Christian Conference to meet at Hank's Chapel Christan Church on the 15th of Nov., 1910

Information is hereby given that arrangements are made by the church to meet all who attend the Conference, and provide homes for them during the session; and that they will be met by the Committee at Pittsboro, N. C., at 6 o'clock, P. M., the 14th day of Nov 1910, whether coming by railway or private conveyance, and homes provided for them.

It is desired that the delegates be appointed by the churches at an early day, so that notices can be given in good time.

Respectfully,
S. M.Holt.

Pittsboro, N. C., Sept. 26th 1910

THE CHRISTIAN SUN.

Founded 1844 by Elder Daniel W. Kerr.
Organ of the Southern Christian
Convention.

Entered at the postoffice at Greensboro, N. C., as second-class matter.

Terms of Subscription.

One Year $1.50
Six Months .... .75
Four Months .... .50
Advertising rates given on application.

J. O. Atkinson, Editor and Publisher.

Important Notice.—As readers will
see, The Christian Sun is now published
at Greensboro, N. C. The office of publication there is 302½ South Elm Street
Our editorial office, however, remains at
Elon College, N. C., to which all letters
and communications to the Editor should
be addressed, as heretofore.

CALENDAR OF CONFERENCES

Time and place of meeting of the
Conferences yet to be held in 1910 are
as follows:

Albama: Pleasant Grove, Tuthday,
October 18, 10 o'clock, a. m. Rev. G. D.
Hunt, Pres., Wadley, Ala. J. W. Payne,
Secty, Wedowee, Ala., F. D., 2.

Georgia and Alabama: Columbus, Ga,
Tuesday, Oct. 25, 7:30, p. m. Rev. H.
W. Elder, Pres., Richland, Ga., J. F.
Hill, Jr., Secty, Box 64 Phoenix, Ala.

Eartern Virginia: Main St. Church,
Berkely, Va.,Tuesday, November 1. Hour
to be appointed by Program Committee.
Rev. N. S. Newman, Pres., Holland, Va.,
Rev. I. W. Johnson, Secty., Suffolk, Va.

Eastern North Carolina: New Elam,
Wednesday, November 9, 10 o'clock a. m
Rev. Jas. L. Foster, Pres., Elon College,
N. C. Rev. W. C. Wicker, Secty;, Elon
College, N. C.

Western North Carolina: Hank's Chapel, Tuesday, November 15, 10:30 o'clock
a. m. Rev. L. I. Cox, Pres. Elon College,
N C. Rev J. W. Patton, Secty., Elon College, N .C.

North Carolina & Virginia: Pleasant
Grove,- (Va). Tuesday, November 22,9:
10 a. m. Prof. W. A. Harper, Pres.,Elon
College. N. C., Prof. W. P. Lawrence,
Secty., Elon College, N. C.

.. THE FAITHFUL SERVANT.

Well done, thou good and faithful servant: thou hast been faithful over a few
things, I will make thee ruler over many
things: enter thou into the joy of thy
lord.—Matt. 25: 21. (Golden text for
Sunday, Oct. 9).

It is not given every one to be great,
rich, powerful in the world, famous
among men. But it is given to every

one who will to be faithful. And that
is better. This is one of the glories of
the Bible and of the gospel: the best
promises are not to the few but to the
many—to all who will comply with conditions and receive them.

The one qualification is that of being
faithful, keeping on, doing the best one
can. The man of five talents was not
blest because he had many: the man of
one talent was not cursed because he
had only one. The blessing and the
curse were on other grounds than these.
The man of five was blest because he
had gone on and had been faithful. The
man of one talent was cursed because
he had not gone on and had not done
his best. The one had been faithful, the
other had been faithless. The one had
been courageous and had not lost hope.
The other was cowardly, gave up, was
afraid, and so had lost out.

It is not required of all to do great
things. It is required of all that they
do the best they can.

The great bulk of this world's work
is done, not by the five and ten talented
persons, but by the one and two talented persons. Nine times out of ten
the one who tugs and tries and keeps
on trying finally accomplishes more than
the daring, bright, brilliant, ready fellow who does not have to try and try
and try again.

The real heroes of every day lfe are
the quiet, honest, earnest faithful citizens who, without praise or applause,
go on in the even tenor of their way,
striving earnestly to do the best they
can, to meet and to conquer the every
day trials and difficulties and remain
faithful in the home, in the field, in the
shop, faithful to their church, their
calling as followers of the most high
God.

The reward does not depend at all
upon the number of talents one has, but
upon the faithfulness with which one
has used the talent given him. One
may consider oneself small, poor, needy,
ignorant, of little consequence, of no influence. God does not so consider or
estimate any one, save that one who
has not used the talent given.

Every one should labor knowing always that the all-seeing eye of God is
upon him and his effort. A current
magazine carries this incident:

"The writer has entertained himself
watching distant people through a telescope. He may have been sweeping a
hillside, when suddenly he detects a
man. He watches him at work, mowing
the field, sharpening the scythe, mopping
his brow, stopping to rest, engaging conversation with a passing neighbor, finally
turning home for noon or night. The

man had not the slightest idea that any
eye had been upon him; and yet in the
court the watcher could have sworn testimony as to his conduct. Sir Walter
Raleigh in his prison cell could at any
moment turn to a small hole in the wall
and there see a human eye watching his
every movement. Thou God seest me."

THERE IS A CURE.

Charity and Children, editorially, asks
and answers as follows:

"Is there any cure for a confirmed
drunkard? A man of our acquaintance,
well on in years, who was a common
drunkard for years, made a bright profession of religion and joined the church.
He struggled against his besetting sin
and seemed to be victorious. For a year
he was an enthusiastic church member
and instituted family worship, gathered
his happy family about him each evening in grateful prayer. The tempter
came along and he forgot his vows and
yielded. For a month he has been wallowing in the ditch."

This is only an instance, Brother Johnson, and one swallow does not make a
summer. There is a cure for the confirmed drunkard, a balm in Gilead, a
healing and a saving power yet operative
in the world. There are thousands today
living sober, happy, triumphant lives,
who in years past were "confirmed
drunkards". They realized their lost,
ruined and undone condition, and yielded
their hearts, lives, souls to God. And
God saved them—saved them from themselves, their appetites, their ruinous career. We have seen scores and scores
of such. Let Bro. Johnson go to the
McAuley Mission, on Water Street, New
York and there he will learn that which
he already knows, that there is a cure
for the confirmed drunkard. For
"where sin abounded grace did much
more abound."

A Record With A Meaning.—I see
from the papers that Rev. C. L. Goodell, D. D., pastor of Calvary Methodist
Church, New York City, has received into church membership, by letter and on
confession, three thousand, seven hundred members during the past six years.
That is a record that has a meaning.
Calvary is one of the "big" and "fashionable," and "leading" churches of
the metropolis. We heard Dr. Goodell
say that he hesitated a long time before
accepting the work there, and that he
was very strongly advised not to accept;
that his method was evangelical, that he
sought members every Sunday, and
preached the old, old gospel in the plain
and practical way. That a big city
church had been, and was the preacher's

grave yard, and Calvary had buried, or had sent to uselessness a great many preachers already. Still Dr. Goodell accepted. And he was a David that did not try to fight in Saul's armor. He carried his old methods, his evangelism, his hunger for the conversion of souls at every service, into his new and great city charge. And Calvary, instead of burying Dr. Goodell has made him famous and useful. He still prays and pleads for and expects conversions at every service, and his expectations are almost always realized. There is nothing on this earth that can take the place of the good old gospel story. And congregations are falling away and church doors being closed up not because their preachers are telling the old, old story, but because they are trying to tell some new-fangled issue of foolishness.

SUFFOLK LETTER.

Weeks have passed since this letter appeared in the Sun and no doubt without loss to any reader or any interest.

I spent three weeks in August at home with my family on the farm: one of those weeks I attended Rev. J. W. Patton's meeting at Oak Level where I preached once and Rev. W. G. Clements the remainder of the time. I like brother Clements' sermons because of ther originality, their uniqueness, and their simplicity. He preaches the gospel in his own way. The meeting was good. The preachers spent one night with us and we enjoyed their company. I think the company of a preacher is a benediction to any home and the pity is that time is too short for successful pastoral visitations. The fireside conversation, the evening family prayer, the great themes that come up for discussion, all inspire the family life with experiences that become resources of satisfaction for all the future.

The first week in September I assisted Rev. H. H. Butler in a meeting at Mount Carmel in Isle of Wight County. I was an all-day dinner-on-the-ground meeting. Great congregations, great dinners. There were 30 converts; 29 joined the church the last day. This church had its origin in a Sunday-school conducted by the sainted Major I. W. Duck whose portrait graces the walls of the new house of worship. Rev. M. B. Barett was the first pastor and his portrait hangs just behind the pulpit. Rev. J. T. Kitchen was the second pastor and Rev. H. H. Butler is the present and beloved shepherd of that good flock. It was the hottest week of the summer when this meeting was held, but

it was not too hot for the presence of the Lord to fill the house of the Lord. Bro. Butler is of the evangelistic type, full of emotion, resourceful in anecdote, untiring in zeal, and knows how to move the people.

The third week in September I assisted Rev. N. G. Newman in a meeting at Holland, Va. Services in afternoon and at night each day. Congregations large and attentive. Ten converts and ten united with the church; one additional convert on Sunday when meeting closed. This meeting was remarkable for the small number of unconverted for a congregation of four hundred.

The village was burned down some months ago and is now being rebuilt in brick and the business houses, when completed, will compare favorably with city stores, It means a revival of business and so business and religion are both revived with good prospects.

Brother N. G. Newman is the careful and painstakng pastor of the Holland Church and of the Holy Neck Church and occupies the nice parsonage owned by these churches jointly. He is one of our scholarly, methodical ministers whose sermons contain meat for men and milk for babes and is winning his way into the hearts of his parishioners by loving them and serving them faithfully.

May I be allowed to remark that we are approaching times when the minister of the Gospel has his largest opportunity. The education of the people increases the demand for thoroughly equipped preachers and the increase of wealth bears on the conscience of men so that remuneration will be adequate to good service. It is a mistake on the part of parents or young men to regard living prospects as poor for the minister. No field of service has a brighter future than that of the ministry; but no half-prepared, half-surrendered, half-hearted man can fill the requirement. The whole head, the whole heart, the whole life and then reward for the whole man. With thirty years of experience I would not exchange results with any other class. I have more than their support, I have their confidence and their love and that is more than money, though money is a great and a responsible possession.

W. W. Staley.

ELON COLLEGE NOTES.

—Revs. L. I. Cox and J. O. Cox conducted a good meeting at Monticello last week.

—Rev. Dr. Newman preached an excel-

lent sermon from the College pulpit last Sunday.

—Mr. C. J. Felton, a ministerial student from the Eastern Virginia Conference, conducted a Y. M. C. A. meeting Saturday evening of genuine spiritual uplift.

—Rev. J. Lee Johnson, a ministerial student of the Eastern North Carolna Conference conducted an interesting Christian Endeavor meeting Sunday evening.

—Mrs. Susie Holland and son, Mr. H. H. Holland, and Mrs. Dr. J. E. Rawls and little daughter, Ann, all of Suffolk, Va., who had spent some days here recuperating, left for their home Thursday afternoon.

—Mrs. Harry Trotman and two children, of Churchland, Va., left on the four o'clock train for their home Thursday, going by way of Raleigh and Suffolk at which latter place Mrs. Trotman and children purpose to spend some time. Their little daughter, Mary Sou, for the benefit of whose health Mrs. Trotman brought her here early in September was much improved.

—Professor and Mrs. Amick had for guests several days last week Professor Amick's brother and his wife from Princeton, West Virginia.

—Miss Ellen Watson who has been at Tryon in the mountains of Western North Carolina for her health since last spring, returned home Saturday on the afternoon train. She is still in feeble health.

—The Elon Banking and Trust Company have let the contract for a new bank building to be constructed of Walnut Cove brick on the corner lot diagonally across the railway from the passenger station. Mr. J. C. McAdams is the contractor, and work began today (Monday) on the lot preparatory to the erection of the brick building. The interior is to be neatly finihed and furnished, and the vault to be constructed of white pressed brick.

—The enrollment in the College is now 193.

—The Executive Committee of the Board of Trustees were in session in the President's office Friday. This committee consists of President Moffitt, Rev. J. W. Wellons, Dr. G. S. Watson, Rev. Dr. P. H. Fleming, of Burlington, N. C., and Mr. K. B. Johnson, of Cardenas, N. C. The Committee attended to some business matters connected with the College, and approved the movement of the Y. M. C. A. to erect a gymnasium, for which building the Association now has subscriptions a little above $300.00   W. P. Lawrence.

THE CHRISTIAN ORPHANAGE DEPARTMENT.

CHILDREN'S PAGE.

The Band of Cousins.

Jas. L. Foster, Supt., Elon College.
J. O. Atkinson, Chr. Board of Trustees, Elon College, N. C.
O. L. Barnes, Treas., Elon College, N. C.

He that hath pity upon the poor lendeth unto the Lord; and that which he hath given will he pay him again.— Prov. 19: 17.

Amt. Brought Forward $1,736.44
Dues.
Nannie Benton .... $ .10
Blanche Franks .... .05
Bettie Franks .... .05
Dwight Franks .... .05
Noma Franks .... .05
Numa Franks .... .05
Monthly S. S. Offerings.
Auburn, N. C., ... .81
3rd Christian S. S., Norf. 7.93
Lambert's Point, Va. 4.40
Howard's Chapel, N. C. 1.00
Special Offering.
F. M. Carlton, Durham,. 6.50
M. H. Hayes, Norlina, .. 1.00
Mrs Rosa Morton,
Burlington, N. C., ... .20
Miss Adeline Wallace,
Union Ridge, N. C., ... 1.00
E. R. Rascoe, Un Rdg. .... .50
Amt. 37th week $23.69
Total $1,760.13

My Dear Children:

No one hundred dollars to report this week, but perhaps this fall several more may come in. We are anxious that all debt be wiped out and Jan. 1911 find us free to make improvements and comforts which are soo needed. We can do this, friends, if every one who is interested will make their Thanksgiving Offering all that they possibly can.

Our children have started to school and imagine, mothers, you have 3 or 4 to get ready, when 35 (our baby boy is not going) start out! Well, they are very much interested and we hope will make good grades this year. If any little girl or boy has second hand Readers Graded Classics Nos. 1, 2, 3, or 4 which they are not going to use we would be glad to have them. Another thing we'd like to have, friends, and that is some good substantial school hats for our children this winter. Anything in this line will be appreciated. Good crop of peas etc., so far and friends very leberal to donate wheat. They do not mean that our children shall lack bread. We were at Union, Alamance, last Sunday with Rev. J. W. Holt, and after the

morning sermon, we talked wheat for a few minutes—and as a result of four minutes "wheat-threshing" we left Bro. Holt gathering up the "tole" and had received about twenty-two bushels, with others to see. Thus we are expecting the 100 bushels necessary to run us from the three churches, Bethlehem, Union, and Pleasant Hill, Alamance, N. C. That will be fine. Our boys and four of the girls gathered 4000 lbs. of clay, peas last week in 3½ days. We have cut 12 acres of corn with four more to take tomorrow. We have 7 acres of young feed corn which is now in the roasting ear. Our cotton is beginning to open nicely. Turnips almost a failure. Don't forget winter hats for the girls and also for the boys—Give us a grand rally next week?

Fondly yours,

Uncle Jim.

———

Greensboro, N. C., Sept. 26, 1910.
Dear Uncle Jim:

I bring my dime for September. I hope all the cousins are having a good time. I am going to school and am in the fifth grade. It will soon be time for the fair. Hope the cousins will all go and have a good time. I will close for this time.

Your niece,
Nannie Benton.

School time with us too, now, Nannie and all the children are enjoying it.

———

Raleigh, N. C., Sept. 24, 1910.
Dear Uncle Jim:

We will send our love and dues for Sept.

We will answer Warner's question, there are four books in the New Testament, that have only one chapter each.

Your nephews and nieces,
Blannie, Bettie, Dwight, Noma and Numa Franks.

It pays to go searching the good old Book, doesn't it, children? Wish we had lots of the cousins to read and ask questions.

NOTES.

Bethlehem.

Our meeting commenced at Bethlehem 2d Sunday in Sept., and closed on Friday afternoon, lasting not quite a week. The church was greatly revived, built up and made, we trust, much stronger for the Master. There were 25 or 30 professions and renewals and about 17 united with the church. Rev. M. L. Bryant of Norfolk, Va. did the preaching to the delight and edification of our people. The Lord bless Bro. Bryant and may he live long to work for

the Master. Our cause is growing at Bethlehem and we need more room for our people. We hope to have sometime in the future a larger house of worship.

Mt. Carmel.

Our meeting closed at Mt. Carmel Friday afternoon before the 2d Sunday. We had a fine meeting—some 30 or 40 professions, 29 united with the church and about 26 were baptized. Here we have a very large and good house of worship. We feel grateful to the Master for the house of worship and the good work accomplished at this place. Rev. W. W. Staley, D. D., did the preaching, and it was fine from the beginning to the end. Our people were delighted with the doctor, and hope he will live to be with them again.

Antioch.

Our meeting closed at Antioch on Friday before the 4th Sunday in Sept. Half day meeting, afternoon. We had a fine meting. Rev. J. T. Kitchen, of Windsor, did the preaching. Bro. Kitchen was at his best and our people were delighted to have him with them. The meeting was fine from the beginning to the end. The pastor enjoyed beyond expression the presence of Bro. K., as they were students together before entering the ministry. The Lord bless dear Bro. Kitchen and may he have many more years to work for the cause of the Master.

Ingram.

The Lord willing, I will be with Rev. S. B. Klapp at Ingram ten days or more in the revival work. The meeting commences Wednesday after the first Sunday in Oct. They are expecting to have all-day services for 8 or 10 days. We are looking forward for a gracious revival of religion at that place. May they prepare the way for the coming of the Lord.

Newport News.

I am also expecting to be with Rev. M. W. Butler at Newport News week after the 3rd Sunday in Oct. We trust that the good people over there with their pastor will fully prepare themselves for the fight that they may gain a glorious voctory over the evil one and capture many for Christ and His cause.

H. H. B.

CHRISTIAN SUN TO ENLARGE.

The Christian Sun, edited by our friend, Dr. J. O. Atkinson will be enlarged to the regular standard four column, sixteen page size, the middle of October. The Sun is one of the leading denominational papers of the State and stands high in the estimation of the newspaper fraternity of the State. Dr. Atkuson is a brilliant and forcible writer, popular throughout the State, and his many friends, and the large number of readers of the Sun will be glad to learn that he is to make the paper the standard and size, and in keeping with the character and standing of his periodical.

The Burlington News will publish the Sun after the 15th of October, when the paper will be enlarged.—Editor Crowson in Burlington News, Sept. 28.

NOTICE.

At the Southern Christian Convention I was appointed the committee of one to arrange for the transportation of delegates to the American Christian Convention.

In order to act intelligently in the matter, it will be necessary for me to know how many will attend. Hence, this notice is a request that all persons who expect to attend notify me at once.

S. M. Smith,

Naval Y. M. C. A., Norfolk, Va.

AIR OFFICERS.

A French author writes: "Only two years ago Wilbur Wright astonished the whole world with a machine that could fly in the true sense of the word; the French government, with characteristic foresight, had offered Mr. Wright the use of the military camp to carry on his experiments." The French author says further that some experiments in France, under the auspices of the government, had been tried ten years before with some success, but adds: "It was not, however, until Captain Lucas Gerardville alighted from his first flight as a passenger with Wilbur Wright at Le Mans that the first government order for a military aeroplane was given out, Captain Gerrardville learned to fly, and France had her first militry airman."

Southern Railway

Operating Over 7,000 Miles of Railway.   Quick Route to all Points North, South, East and West.

For Speed, Comfort, Courteous Employees, travel via the Southern Railway.

Rates, Schedules and other information furnished by any of the undersigned.

R. L. VERNON, Trav. Pass. Agt.,   J. H. WOOD, Dist. Pass. Agt.,
    Charlotte, N. C.   Asheville, N. C.

S. H. HARDWICK, P. T. M.,   W. H. TAYLOE, G. P. A.,

Washington, D. C.

IT WILL BE TO YOUR INTEREST

to see us when you want FURNITURE, CARPETS, RUGS, STOVES, or anything in the HOUSE FURNISHING line. We carry the largest stock in this line in Alamance County.

M. B. Smith,

Burlington, N. C.

FOR RENT.

I have a farm to rent at Elon College, —58 acres, with good 6-room house, a good well of water, and out-buildings. This is a chance for some one that wants to educate his children and farm also. I will rent for standing rent one year with privilege of three or five years.

J. J. Lambeth,

Elon College, N. C.

Since then military airmanship has made great strides. Instead of one air officer, France has now twenty. Henry Farman has a school at Chalons Camp, and the aeronautic education of the French Army is going forward in real earnest. On any fine day a number of military areoplanes may be seen in the air at Chalons, and at the Wright School of the Comte de Lambert at Villadoublay." Lieutenants, captains and even generals all want to fly and as fast as the constructors can turn out the machines fresh pupils come forward for instruction.—N. Y. Christan Advocate.

—Here is a cause for disturbance in four very large families. Chicago has published a city directory of its 800,000 families and it is seen there that are 8,000 Johnsons and only 5,300 Smiths. There are only 2,800 Browns and the Jones number is only 2,000.

—Governor Kitchen has appointed B. F. Dixon, Jr. to succeed his late lamented father, B. F. Dixon, Sr. as Auditor of North Carolina. Maj. Dixon was a gallant Confederate soldier and officer, an orator of influence and power, a statesman honored, trusted and esteemed. His untimely death was mourned throughout the State.

RALEIGH & SOUTHPORT RY. CO.

Southbound Daily.

STATIONS	A.M.	P.M.	P.M.
Lv. Raleigh	8:00	1:15	6:35
" Caraleigh	8:10	1:23	6:45
" McCullers	8:35	1:43	7:07
" Willow Springs .	8:52	1:55	7:25
" Varina	9:04	2:05	7:35
" Fuquay Springs .	9:14	2:12	7:45
" Chalybeate	9:35	2:30	8:00
" Kipling	9:40	2:35	8:05
" Cape Fear	9:53	2:46	8:18
" Lillington	10:00	2:53	8:25
" Harnett	10:08	3:01	8:33
" Bunlevel	10:13	3:06	8:38
" Linden	10:23	3:15	8:48
" Lane	10:34	3:25	8:59
" Slocomb	10:39	3:30	9:04
Ar. Fayetteville	11:10	4:00	9:35

Northbound Daily.

	A.M.	P.M.	P.M.
Lv. Fayetteville	8:00	1:00	5:10
" Slocomb	8:28	1:28	5:38
" Lane	8:33	1:32	5:43
" Linden	8:45	1:43	5:54
" Bunlevel	8:55	1:52	6:03
" Harnett	9:01	1:58	6:09
" Lillington	9:11	2:08	6:20
" Cape Fear	9:16	2:13	6:26
" Kipling	9:28	2:24	6:43
" Chalybeate	9:35	2:30	6:49
" Fuquay Springs .	9:50	2:45	7:05
" Varina	10:00	2:52	7:14
" Willow Springs .	10:09	3:02	7:25
" McCullers	10:22	3:15	7:41
" Caraleigh	10:40	3:35	8:06
Ar. Raleigh	10:50	3:45	8:20

YOUNG PEOPLE'S DEPARTMENT.
Exponent of the Young People's Convention,
Christian Church, South.

Watchword;   A Christian Endeavor Society in Every Church; Teacher-Training and Organized Classes in Every Sunday School
W. A. HARPER, Editor and Field Secretary, Elon College, N. C.

[All notes and contributions for this department should be sent to W. A. Harper, Elon College, N. C. All items under this Department not signed are by its Editor and Field Secretary.]

THE YOUNG PEOPLE'S MOVEMENT
In Five Parts. Number IV.
The Relation of the Sunday-school and Young People's Conventions.

The last section of the Constitution has given rise to considerable discussion and misunderstanding. At the risk of tiring the reader I will quote that section of the constitution again in full. It reads as follows:

"Section 9. In order that every phase of our work may be provided for we reccommend further that the officers of our Annual Sunday School Conventions be requested to provide in their programs for Christian Endeavor, Missions, and other lines of work which we represent, and that our Annual Sunday School Conventions operating in the local Conferences."

In the first place note the request that the proper officials of our Sunday School Conventions be requested to give Christian Endeavor, Missions, and the other lines of work represented by the Convention a place in the program. This practically every body among us has done and will no doubt continue to do so, tho we hope that they will give at least a little more time to the Christian Endeavor idea as the Society gets stronger in the bounds of each Convention. In the second place the recommendation is made that our Annual Sunday School Conventions be gradually merged into Young People's Conventions operating in the local Conferences and holding a position and relationship to the general Young People's Convention of our Southern Christian Convention similar and parallel to that occupied by our annual Conferences with reference to the Southern Christian Convention itself. On this point there has been a difference of opinion—respecting the change of name. What we want is the thing, the idea, call it what you will. But it does seem a little odd to have a Christian Endeavor Department to a Sunday School Convention; still, if that is best for our people, I am ready to stand for it as solidly as anyone and so will all those who have the good of of the Young People's Convention at heart.

But this much is certain, unless all our Conventions for Sunday Schools and Christian Endeavor and Missions and so forth can get together on a working basis, our Young People's Convention is dead and will soon need the undertaker and the funeral sermon. We are too small to be divided . Our only hope is in united action. "United we stand, divided we fall" said Benjamin Franklin when the thirteen Colonies, now grown to the great nation we proudly claim as our father-land, were quarreling and warring with each other about which should have precedence and what was best to do. The homely humor and wit of poor Richard got them together and today we see the wisdom of that "get together" policy. Would to God that we may find a Poor Richard among our people, who shall lead us to similar unity and brotherhood and fellowship and co-operation in this Young People's work, when is the hope of our Church, as of every Church!

S. S. LESSON FOR OCT. 9, 1910.
By Dr. W. C. Wicker. . . . . . .
The Last Judgment.
Read Matthew, 25: 31-46.
Golden Text:—Inasmuch as ye have done it unto one of the least of these my brethren, ye have done it unto me. Matt. 25: 40.

Introduction.

Study the Bible for the qualifications of a Christian that fit him for eternal life and see to what extent Christianity is hearing the Word of God, or theorizing and speculating about Christian doctrine and to what extent we as Christians are called upon to do the will of God. Doing His will, doing His commandments, doing service for fellowmen, doing the truths of the gospel until they are woven into habitual character will enable Jesus Christ when He shall come in His glory to say, " Well done, good and faithful servant, enter thou into the joy of thy Lord."

It was on Tuesday, April 4th, A. D. 30, the same day on which the facts of the two preceding lessons were given by Jesus to His disciples. They were still at the Mount of Olives overlooking Jerusalem. Jesus had in retrospect the disobedience of the Jewish race; before Him the great center of Jewish worship and in prospect his condemnation and crucifixion by cruel men. He teaches

the disciples a great truth about service, judgment and reward.

1. The Judgment Day, vs 31-32. When the Son of man, the judge of all the earth, shall come in His glory, in His perfect character revealing itself in all its purity, perfection and beauty to friends and enemies, to the former for approval, and the latter for condemnation, and with Him all the holy angels, ministering spirits, the forces of nature, and the personalities of heaven and earth who co-operate with Him in the advancement of the divine kingdom, He shall come as a king and sit upon the throne of His glory. He shall then gather the whole human race, rich and poor, learned and unlearned, good and bad, saved and unsaved and shall separate them one from another. There shall then be only two well defined classes,—those who love God supremely, who have begun the heavenly life, and who have done the will of the Father and those who have not. There will be many in the first class that were condemned to the second and many in the second who made the world believe they belonged to the first. When the secrets of all hearts are made known there will be no deception and no mistake by the great Judge of all the earth.

They shall be divided as a shepherd divideth his sheep from the goats. They may feed together upon the green pastures of God's mercy and drink from the cool and sparkling water of life while here among men, but then the crisis will come, the dead line will be drawn and there will be a final separation.

II. The Righteous and their Reward, vs. 33-40.

The sheep representing the children of God, possessing a spirit of gentleness, obedience, patience, meekness, submission, affection, service even to the giving of their own life without murmuring for the blessings of others, those who possess and manifest these excellent traits and characteristics of the righteous Christian life shall be placed on His right hand. This is a place of honor and divine favor and protection. They shall be in the secret place of the Most High, under the shadow of his wings where nothing can befall or harm them forever.

Then shall the king say unto them on his right hand, the righteous, "Come, ye blessed of my Father." Those who have been blessed by the wise provision of salvation, touched by the quickening spirit of conviction, saved by pardoning grace, and regenerated by redeeming love and made heirs with Christ, Inherit, receive not by merit or labor or purchase, but as a gracious gift through unmerited love, the kingdom, of heaven, that kingdom that consists of righteousness, peace, and joy in the Holy Ghost and is peopled only by those who are righteous, possessing the rich qualities of divine purpose, Christian spirit, harmonious communion with Christ and have made known His will among men by doing, as well as teaching the truths of the gospel while upon the earth. Such a place as this has been prepared by the wise pre-vision and provision of a loving Father and a compassionate Christ from the foundation of the world. We have not been called into service by chance but the wise and loving Father has planned our lives, prepared us a place in life, a work, a place in His kingdom, an abiding place in His home.

If we have done our work, filled our place in life, He recognizes every service rendered directly to Him, He identifies himself with us in all the sorrows, sufferings and sickness, trials, temptations and tribulations that ever come to us, and service rendered in His spirit for the alleviation, mollification, or mitigation of such sorrows is recognized as service to himself. "Inasmuch as ye have done it unto one of the least of these, my brethren, ye have done it unto me."

III. The Unrighteous and their Doom. vs. 41-46.

The goats representing the wicked, neglectful, heartless or unsympathetic, were placed on the left hand,—a place of dishonor, disgust, banishment, because the goat is stubborn, wanton, wild, intractable and self-willed, not being submissive to their leader and guide. Unto them on the left hand, he said, Depart from me. The purity, spiritual perfection, heavenly character and holy presence of Christ is the most powerful rebuke for, sin, repelling the sin or the sinner from His presence, condemning the sinner as cursed and exiling him into the everlasting fire of torment, condemned conscience, perpetual remorse, agnozing memory of past opportunities unimproved.

"Of all sad words of tongue or pen, The saddest of these, it might have been."

As he reflects upon the past and looks to the future two eternities of gloom, remorse, condemnation, torture, despair and misery roll in upon him like the vapor of smoke of hell closing in upon him.

But this place of torment, this remorseful torture was prepared for the devil and his angels, not for men and mortals made in the image of God, and stamped with the image of Christ, hence the greater gloom for those who so live and neglect Christian duty as to enter upon this experience of eternal doom.

"So live that when the summons comes to join

The innumerable caravan which moves
To that mysterious realm where each shall take

His chamber in the silent halls of death,
Then go not, like the quarry-slave at night

Scourged to his dungeon; but, sustained and soothed

By the unfaltering trust, approach thy grave

Like one who wraps the drapery of his couch

About him, and lies down to pleasant dreams.''

THE SOCIETY AND THE MINISTER.

As Endeavorers we are pledged to support our own church, and it is expected of us that we keep that pledge as far as in us lies.

Sometimes one hears complaints of Endeavorers' not supporting the regular meetings of the church. I think that their support compares well with that of older members; but, apart from this there is no doubt that there is room for improvement.

Attending church must be removed from the plane of religious duties; it must be made a delight:.

Hence the thing to do is not to complain of poor attendance, but to make the services attractive, give the young people something to do and something to work for.

The Iowa Christian Endeavorer says: "The pastor of the strongest Presbyterian church in Rochester, N. Y., was saved in the ministry of that congregation by a body of young people rallying about him when the tide seemed to turn against him with an almost hopeless speed of flow. But they talked it over, a few of them, and determined to 'boost' him in every possible way. They did, and for more than forty years Dr. William R. Taylor has remained at the head of the 'Old Brick Church," universally honored, venerated and loved—all because his young people in the time of dire need came to his aid."

The whole society should be a pastor's aid committee—alwasy ready to do whatever can be done to help. When the machinery is well oiled with mutual love there will be no creaking.

C. E. TOPIC FOR OCT. 8. A FEW SUGGESTIONS.

Forward Steps in Our Society.—Exod. 14: 9-15.

The Scripture: If the leader reads, let him appoint some one else to comment. The comment should be brief—should suggest the misgivings and fears attendant on any new movement in life and the results of always moving forward.

The Leader: The leader's remarks should be very practical. He would do well to show that we advance, not by journeys but by single steps. Let him briefly outline the importantnext step for the society, which should be presented after a Conference with the officers and chairmen of committees; for there cannot be progress without unanimity respecting it.

Question Spurs. (To come in as voluntary participation):

Name one step our Society ought to take. (To several).

What step for improvement can the Look-out Committee take? (Give to the chairman of this committee. Do likewise of each committee in the Society).

What new committee or committees would make the Society more efficient?

How can we have better prayer-meetings?

What shall we do with the late-comers?

Back-setters?

Verse readers?

Absentees?

Long talkers?

Those who won't pray in public?

Those who won't lead the meeting?

What is holding our Society back?

What will put it forward?

Why must we go forward or backward?

Bible Verses. (To come in as voluntary participation):

Call of Abraham, Gen. 12: 1.

We will do His command, Exod. 19: 8.

Willingly with his heart, Exod. 25: 2

Went before the people, Josh. 3: 6.

The Day of Pentecost, Acts 2: 1.

Deacons chosen, Acts 6: 3.

Missionaries called, Acts 13: 2.

His workmanship, Eph. 2: 10.

The Immutability of His counsel, Heb. 6: 17.

Thy will be done, Matt. 6: 10.

Do the will of my Father, Matt 12. 50.

For this purpose, Acts 26: 16.

We are sowers, Matt. 13: 3.

We are grains of mustard seed, Matr. 13: 31.

We are leaven, Matt. 13: 33.

I. Apollos, God, 1 Cor. 3: 6-8.

For Next Time: Your Amusements.

M., Oct. 10. Innocent amusements. 1 Tim. 4: 8.

T., Oct. 11. In the grip of amusement. 1 Cor. 6: 12.

W., Oct. 12. Can others bear it? 1 Cor. 8: 7-13.

T., Oct. 13. A death dance . 1 Cor. 10: 1-7

F., Oct. 14. A peculiar people. 2 Cor. 6: 14-18.

S., Oct. 15. True joy. Ps. 16: 5-11.

S., Topic—Your amusements: do they build up or tear down? Rom. 15: 1-3; Ps. 36: 7-12.

Suggested Program.

1 Prayer and Song Service—10 minutes.

2. Scripture. Comment.

3. Prayer by pastor.

4. Special Music.

5. Leader's Remarks—5 minutes.

6. Song.

7 Voluntary participation in what ever form desired, but including question spurs and Bible verses voluntarily submitted without being specifically called for, interspersed with stanzas of appropriate song.:

8 Prayer—a chain of sentence prayers.

9. Pastor's five minutes.

10. Song. Offering. Aaronicbenediction.

MARRIED.

Williams-Smith.

Near Suffolk, Va., Sept. 16th 1910, at the home of the bride's father, Mr. W. T. Smith, Mr. Hatcher Watson Williams the eldest son of Mr. and Mrs J. T. Williams, who is a very popular and successful young farmer and also one of Elon's students, and Miss Edna Thomas Smith, the very beautiful and accomplished daughter of Mr. and Mrs. W. T. Smith. They are both members of Bethlehem Christian Church and have the best wishes and prayers of their many friends.

H. H. B.

DIED.

Beaton.

At his home near Zuni, Va., August 31, 1910, John H. Beaton, aged 79 years and one day. He made a profession of religion and united with Antioch Church and remained true and faithful until some time after Mt. Carmel Church was established. He then, with his wife and daughter, Effie, united with the church there and became a great help to the cause of the Master

at that place and at his death he was among the most influential and oldest members of that church. He was a true and accepted Mason, a member of Blackwater Lodge No. 134. He was treasurer of his lodge for about 25 years or as long as he was able to attend his lodge meetings. He went through the four years of the Civil War and was wounded in the seven days' fight at Malvern Hill. He belonged to the 16th Va. Regiment, Co. D., the Isle of Wight grays. He leaves to mourn their loss a devoted wife, one sister, Mrs. C. B. Crumpler, of Suffolk, Va., and many nephews and nieces, and many other relatives and devoted friends. His funeral service was conducted by his pastor at his home and his remains were laid to rest by his Masonic brethren in the family cemetery close by the remains of those of his dear children who preceded him several years to the better land. The Lord bless and comfort his dear aged companion, relatives and friends.

H. H. B.

Joyner.

In Norfolk, Va., Aug. 31, 1910, Jas. L. Joyner, the son of Deacon J. E. T. Joyner, aged 27 years, 5 months and one day.

He leaves to mourn their loss a devoted father, step-mother, one own brother, two half brothers, two own sisters and two half sisters. His funeral service was conducted by the pastor at Mt. Carmel Christian Church and his remains laid to rest in the church cemetery. The Lord bless and comfort the dear bereaved ones.

H. H. B.

Gibson.

Whereas God in His infinite wisdom

has taken from us our esteemed friend and brother, John Gibson, Sr.,

Resolved that the church has lost one of her most loyal members and that we will cherish the memory of his devotion to his church.

The wife has lost a devoted husband; his children a loving and affectionate father; the country an esteemed and true citizen.

Resolved, further, that we bow in submission to Him who doeth all things well, and that a copy of these resolutions be placed on our church record, a copy be sent to the family, also to the Christian Sun for publication. By order of the church in conference.

    G. D. Hunt,
    J. M. Welch,
    C. W. Carter, Com.

Archer.

At his home near Exit, Va., Sept. 19, 1910, Aaron Archer, aged 87 years, ten months and 27 days. He was one among the oldest members of Bethlehem Christian Church. He loved his church and attended as long as he was able to do so. He leaves to mourn their loss, one devoted daughter, Mrs. S. J. Saunders, and three grandsons, Mr. Hurley K Saunders, S. A. and Dr. F. W. Archer of Norfolk, Va., and a host of relatives and friends. The funeral services were conducted at Bethlehem by his pastor, and his remains were laid to rest in the church cemetery close beside those of his dear wife and son to await the resurrection morn. The Lord bless and comfort the dear bereaved ones.

H. H. B.

The North Carolina State Fair will be opened by Gov. Kitchen at noon Monday Oct. 17 and will continue till Saturday Oct. 22. This gives promise of being the most largely attended Fair in years.

THE MOTHER OF PHILLIPS BROOKS.

Every true mother of boys—the "comrade" mother who has been her boys' most sympathizing friend and closest chum—experiences a season of heartache and distress when the time comes, as inevitably does in boy development, that confidence seems to be withdrawn and the young sons turn elsewhere for the comfort and understanding hitherto found alone in the mother comrade. To such mothers the mother of Phillips Brooks writes out her own deep experience:

"There is an age when it is not well to follow or question your boy too closely. Up to that time you may carefully instruct and direct him, you are his best friend; he is never happy unless the story of the day has been told; you must hear about his friends, his school, all that interests him must be your interest. Suddenly these confidences cease the affectionate son becomes reserved and silent, he seeks the intimate friendship of other lads, he goes out, he is averse to telling where he is going or how long he will be gone. He comes in and goes silently to his room.

"All this is a startling change to the mother, but it is also her opportunity to practice wisdom by loving and praying for and absolutely trusting her son. The faithful instruction and careful training during his early years the son can never forget; that is impossible. There fore trust not only your heavenly Father but your son. The period of which I speak appears to come to one in which the boy dies and the man is born; his individuality rscs up before him, and he is dazed and almost overwhelmed by his first consciousness of himself. I have always believed that it was then the Creator was speaking with my sons, and that it was good for their souls to be left alone with him, while I, their mother, stood trembling, praying and waiting, knowing that when the man was developed from the boy I should have my sons again, and there would be a deeper sympathy between us."—Interior.

—The population of Richmond, Va., increased during the decade just past from 85,050 to 127,628 which was 50.1 percent. This is gratifying growth indeed.

—The Chinese, in some provinces, are on the verge of an outbreak similar to the Boxer uprising and the lives of foreigners are in jeopardy. There are mutterings and discontent among the Chinese and the out break is much feared.

Elon College.
Co-educational.

The Only Institution of higher education fostered by the Southern Christian Convention.

Modern in Equipment, Steam Heat, Electric Lights, Baths, Sewerage, Elegant new buildings.

Four Degree Courses. Special Courses for Teachers, approved and endorsed by the State Superintendent of Public Instruction.

A High Grade Institution whose graduates are admitted to the Graduate Department of all the great universities without examination.

Maintains Excellent Music, Art, Elocution, Business and Preparatory Departments.

A Faculty of Thirteen Specialists, with a successful record of twenty years.

Has all the Advantages of city life with none of its disadvantages. Situated in the delightful hill country of North Carolina, famed for its healthfulness, pure water, and high moral tone.

Elon College has done more to build up the Christian Church than any institution ever yet commissioned by our people.

Terms Very Moderate. For Catalogue or other information, address:

EMMETT L. MOFFITT, President, or

W. A. HARPER, Dean,
Elon College, N. C.

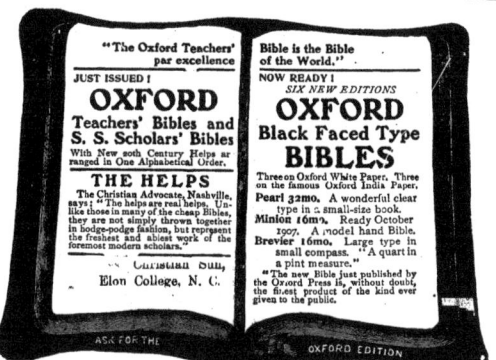

REMEMBER: That we guarantee satisfaction and sell to you cheaper than the publisher and dealers do. Our business is by mail and express and prices quoted are the prices of goods delivered to you. We can furnish you the Oxford, or the Holman Teacher's Bible at prices ranging from $1.35 to $4.00. Send for our catalogue or write us what you want. Address

THE CHRISTIAN SUN, Elon College, N. C.

HELP NEEDED.

The Supt. of the Christian Orphanage would be pleased to correspond with any strong, healthy, competent woman who may desire to work and who would accept a position as help in the kitchen, and similar work at the Orphanage. Write at once to Jas. L. Foster, Supt. Elon College, N. C.

—One of the big days of the State Fair this year will be "Good Roads Day," Wednesday October 19th. Road machinery of all kinds, the most modern and up-to-date that has be devised as a result of the recent agitation for good roads, will be on exhibition and working. This Good Roads demonstration has been worked up for a long time, and with the utmost diligence, and it will be one of the chief educational features of the Fair of 1910. The plan is to provide stone on the ground for crushing purposes, and a space 400 by 30 feet has been laid off for the construction in sections by different lines of machinery exhibited, so that each manufacturer can demonstrate his system of road making before the very eyes of the visitors.

—In the automobile races for the Vanderbilt cup in New York last Saturday four persons were killed and twenty injured.

—Iceland, about half the size of Missouri, has no jail, no penitentiary; there is no court, and only one policeman. Not a drop of alcoholic liquor is made on the island, and its 78,000 people are total abstainers, since they will not permit any liquor to be imported. There is not an illiterate person on the island, not a child ten years old unable to read, the system of public schools being practically perfect.—S. C. Tharp, Pretty Prarie, Kansas.

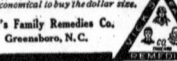

CPSIA information can be obtained
at www.ICGtesting.com
Printed in the USA
BVHW060348061118
532207BV00028B/5672/P

9 780243 083527